Serenity

Serenity

Inspirations by Karen Casey
Author of *Each Day a New Beginning*

HAZELDEN®

Hazelden
Center City, Minnesota 55012-0176

1-800-328-0094
1-651-213-4590 (Fax)
www.hazelden.org

Library of Congress Cataloging-in-Publication Data

Casey, Karen.
   Serenity : inspirations / by Karen Casey.
      p. cm.
   ISBN-13: 978-1-59285-409-7 (softcover)
   ISBN-10: 1-59285-409-5 (softcover)
   1. Peace of mind—Religious aspects—Meditations. I. Title.
   BL627.55.C37 2007
   158.1'28—dc22   2006049740

Editor's note
The text in this book has been adapted from *A Life of My Own: Meditations on Hope and Acceptance*.

11   10   09   08   07   6 5 4 3 2 1

Cover and interior design by David Spohn
Typesetting by Prism Publishing Center

Introduction

The attainment of serenity may seem impossible to many of us, whether we're facing serious life challenges or just the annoyances that plague daily life. Often, our greatest worries are based on what we can't control and what we can't change. Those worries can be related to our jobs, our health, or the well-being of loved ones. When so many problems pile up, we can be left feeling resentful and bitter.

Nurturing a sense of serenity is possible, however, when we become willing to detach from the things we have no control over. Detachment is, in fact, a profound spiritual challenge for many of us, because we carry the illusion that we are somehow responsible for fixing the problems of the people we care most about, whether they are our family members, co-workers, or neighbors.

There is an alternative to constantly defending this illusion of control. And that alternative is simply turning our problems and worries over to a Higher Power. That doesn't mean we stop being responsible adults, but it does mean we begin to cultivate a sense of trust that God will take care of our loved ones and that God does have a plan for all the people and circumstances in our lives.

Serenity is possible when we embrace the idea that our Higher Power has a plan for everyone, including ourselves.

We can look forward to a serene outlook on every encounter today if we remember that God will be along for the ride. So much of what was expected of us in years past filled us with dread because we thought we were alone. We feared we couldn't cope with our situations. Now we have hope, serenity, and faith that all is well, and all will always be well, because our Higher Power is as close as our breath.

Most of us don't know what we want to be doing a year or even a month from now. When we are called upon to make decisions that commit us to a certain path in the future, we shudder. Will we be allowed to change our minds?

No decision has to bind us forever. Our decisions today will be for this day only. We can change our minds tomorrow.

I will find as much joy in today as I want to find. I will try to remember that each moment is sacred and full of promise.

I will relish my moments with God today.
They will help me in every circumstance.
I'm never alone as long as I remember God.

Having problems is the path to the growth and serenity we seek. When we turn to God for guidance, and trust in Him, we see the problem transformed into an opportunity. To acknowledge life as being filled with opportunity rather than problems is a tiny shift in perspective that gives us huge rewards.

Hope makes it possible for us to expect more positive outcomes to our problems. It's so often true that what we expect is just what we get. Looking on the bright side of life can't make our struggles worse!

"Let go"
are tiny words with huge rewards.
If I want to, I can give up my
attempts to control someone today.
Peace will be my reward.

I will open my heart to God's wisdom today and find help for whatever troubles me.

Because we doubt that God will tell us how to handle the circumstances facing us, we aggressively move ahead, making decisions that are often not in sync with God's will and certainly not in our long-term best interests. We complicate our lives unnecessarily.

On occasion, our problems seem overwhelming, and we don't know where to turn. Perhaps our job is stressful, our health is failing, or the pain of living with a troubled family member is becoming more difficult. But many of us face no truly threatening situations, and we still have problems. Being alive, being human, means having experiences that trouble us.

I feel hopeful, because I believe that God is taking care of me according to His plan for my life. Praying for knowledge of God's will for me is a prayer that always gets answered.

I am so lucky that I have a Higher Power that I can call on today. I can be certain that I'll be taken care of.

Character defects cause our conflicts with others, trigger our self-pity, set us up for unrealistic expectations, exaggerate the "molehills," and minimize the joys. It's a fact, clear and simple, that any unhappiness is attributable to our own perception, our own response to the people and activities surrounding us.

Being hopeful is an attainable attitude. Coming to believe in the presence of a Higher Power in our lives will accelerate our acceptance of hope. With the help of God and our friends, we will firmly come to know that we are never alone, that all is well. We will experience the hope we hear in the voices of others.

Today I can become more positive by regularly putting myself in the company of friends who have hope.

I am slowly learning that giving up control, giving up worry, and giving up outcomes give me profound relief.

What we come to understand from the shared wisdom of other people is that a caring God, however we define God, will give us comfort, direction, and the sense that we are no longer *ever* alone. No longer do we need to lose sleep over any situation. Our reliance on the guidance we have been promised will take the worry out of our lives, giving us time to accomplish goals that have been long forgotten.

Letting go of the outcomes of all experiences, even those that involve us, frees our minds from the needless worry that keeps us stuck. The more we focus on a problem, our own or someone else's, the bigger it gets.

*Telling a trusted friend about
a problem will make this day more
productive. And the problem
may get solved, too!*

*I have nothing to fear today or any day
as long as I let God take charge of me and
all the circumstances in my life.*

I want to feel peaceful today. Asking for knowledge of God's will and then following it will make me peaceful.

Becoming willing to pause long enough to ask ourselves what God would want us to do in a specific situation, and then doing it, assures us that God's will, not our will, is in charge. We'll then feel peace.

I can choose to be serene and hopeful about every detail of my life.

My affirmation for today is
"I can be as hopeful and happy
as I decide to be."

Every day we encounter people who exude peacefulness. We wonder how they attained their peace. If we watch them closely, we'll notice how accepting they are of people. They seem not to be bothered by conflicting opinions, unconcerned by decisions that don't affect them, and uninterested in controlling situations that involve others.

Worrying distorts our perceptions of an experience. It takes away the spontaneous joy we might have known. Even more troubling, it compromises our ability to be present in the moment. When we worry, we aren't in touch with what is happening in the present. Meanwhile, our lives can pass us by.

We are learning that at the right time, in the right way, God will change what needs changing in others' lives. Prayer is very helpful. In particular, it quiets our minds. But God's timetable is out of our hands.

Shouldering any problem alone,

grave or small, is

never necessary.

Problems are opportunities for growth. They let us experience the wisdom of other people when we ask for help. They assure us a better connection to our Higher Power if we want it. And they give us chances to practice inner silence and find the place where all answers ultimately reside. Going within offers us profound calm, the love and the secure comfort of our Higher Power.

Willfulness and serenity cannot coexist. I can give my will to God today. Every time I open my mouth to correct or control someone else, I'll stop and ask God to take over for me.

Daily we are in situations that can erupt in conflict. How we handle ourselves, particularly our thoughts, contributes to the conflict's escalation or defusion.

I will know that all is well today
if I turn to God for whatever help I need.
I don't need to do anything alone.

We will know greater joy and peace when we rely on our Higher Power for the solutions to our problems. Alone, we don't have all the answers. We don't need to. We will be told what we need to know if we ask for the guidance that we've been promised.

I can live in the present moment. With determination I can let my worries go.

Believing that all people have a Higher Power watching over them gives us some relief from the worry that haunts us. We cannot change others. We cannot control any action that another person takes. But we can accept other people as they are and decide to take control of our own thinking and actions.

Making a decision to
let God give us guidance
eases our burdens.

Being human means making mistakes. No doubt we could have been better parents, better lovers, better employees, surely better children. But we were good enough! Forgiving ourselves for our past transgressions will free us to find more serenity in our present lives.

We can handle everything as it is, just for today. Living just for today will give us a fresh outlook on every day as it unfolds. Few things will overwhelm us when we keep our focus on today.

When I feel fear today, I'll turn to God for the help I've been promised.

I will live today moment by moment.
I will be prepared for the future when it comes.

Because we don't know just where God is taking us, we can't possibly anticipate all that we'll need to know. That's where God's plan comes in. We will be given our lessons when the time is right. We won't be led into situations we're unprepared for. And we will trust that each circumstance we do face is necessary and part of our unfolding.

We can never know, absolutely, what God's plan for our life is. Yet we can trust that there is one and that we are being watched over. Almost every day an experience troubles us. Maybe it's a phone call from a friend or a criticism from a boss. So quickly we judge its meaning for our life. But from the experiences we were certain we couldn't live through, we garnered important knowledge and growth. Today's experiences will be understood in time as well.

My journey will be what I make it today.
I will detach with love.

When I wonder, "Why me?"
let me remember how lucky I am to
still be fulfilling God's plan.

Our lives are frightening at times. Conflict with significant people causes fear of abandonment. A new job triggers fear of inadequacy. Perhaps we simply had a bad dream that seemed far too real. Any of these reasons might push our "fear" button, but we *can* handle anything if we ask God for help and take it one day at a time.

Today will be what we make it. Regardless of the weather, the kinds of work to be done, the personalities crossing our paths, we'll feel joy and peace if that is our choice.

I can give up my controlling
ways if I'm willing to accept that
a Higher Power might know
what's best.

Nothing can really frighten us if we live our lives one breath at a time. Breathing in the presence of our Higher Power extinguishes the flame of fear that worry triggers.

Guidance is a gift I can expect when I turn to my Higher Power. I will be more serene today if I follow the guidance that comes to me through prayer and meditation.

We've had lots of pain in our lives. We'll no doubt experience more pain, but accepting help will make the experiences tolerable, and we won't be defeated. Humbly asking our Higher Power for help guarantees we'll get it.

Fear won't trouble me today if I remember that God is my companion.

The negative experiences in my past served a purpose. I will come to believe in their value, and I will trust that all my experiences today are right for me now. My Higher Power will help me through them.

How lucky I am to have discovered, at last, the peace that comes with surrendering. There is a plan for my life. There is a plan for my companion's life too. And for my friends' and associates' lives. None of us has been left out of the divine plan. Now I can breathe easier, knowing God will take care of all those people I tried to manage but couldn't.

Conflict can result from trying to change a person or situation that we don't like. And conflict causes stress and agitation, both of which limit our lives. They steal our ability to be open to opportunities for growth and change. Acceptance frees us.

Some of us exaggerate small setbacks, making our lives far more complicated than necessary. Instead, we need to nurture a positive outlook. The wise among us say, "It's all in how you look at it."

I can have either peaceful or stressful interactions with people I meet today. What develops depends on how I behave.

We can anticipate the day we have awakened to with a feeling of promise or dread. There will be situations, no doubt, that we'd rather not face. Petty irritations may shadow us part of the day, but most likely we'll find a few circumstances to laugh over. We will find more of these circumstances if we so choose. The attitude we have today will determine the quality of our day.

Honestly reflecting on our past convinces us that most situations we worried ourselves sick over didn't turn out as badly as we had imagined. Or if they did, our Higher Power helped us get through them. Generally, we worry about what we anticipate might happen tomorrow or next month. Our focus is seldom on this day. If we could develop the willingness to live just the twenty-four hours before us, we'd hardly ever worry.

Today is it. I can't be sure of tomorrow or next year. Thus I will keep my focus on the treasures God gives me today. They are meant for my special journey.

When life isn't unfolding as we had anticipated, it's because God has other plans. Getting used to this idea will make fear a rare emotion. And we'll have much more time to enjoy the pleasures of life.

Life is a process that includes problems that can't always be easily resolved. How refreshing to learn that we don't have to resolve every conflict. We can simply let conflicts be and focus on peaceful images and think loving thoughts instead. We can be certain that we won't remember most of today's troubles tomorrow unless we want to.

I deserve to feel good about my life today. I have many blessings that I take for granted. I'll think about them today, and my attitude will reflect my gratitude.

We can have freedom from fear. All we have to do is accept our Higher Power as our daily companion.

Blessings abound in our lives.
We need to remember the tiny joys:
a call from a friend, a smile from a
stranger, the beauty of nature.

Acknowledging our negative attitude is the first step to discovering happiness. We can't deny the difficulty inherent in many circumstances, nor the pain that accompanies losses. We can, however, choose to see our experiences, no matter how traumatic, as lessons moving us closer to the enlightened state God intends for us.

Not letting other people know what's troubling us causes the problem to trouble us even more. "Secrets keep us stuck," say the wise ones on our journey. Sharing what's on our minds with a friend gives that person an opportunity to help us develop a better perspective. On the other hand, staying isolated with our worries exaggerates them.

Because I used to worry far too much, life wasn't as fun as I'm now capable of making it. Today won't be a repeat of the old days. No matter what happens, I need not worry. God will take care of me.

*With my Higher Power's help,
I will get hope and relief today in all my
experiences, no matter how troubling.*

What freedom we feel when we don't have to figure out every detail of our lives. If we wonder how to handle our relationships with difficult people, God will show us. When a loved one gets into trouble, God will help us let that person solve the problem. On those days when we feel afraid and don't know why, we can remember God's presence and gain courage and comfort.

For some of us, fear is a constant companion. The hot ball of anxiety in the stomach becomes a way of life, and we never expect to feel any other way. We worry about the well-being of our loved ones, we worry about keeping our jobs, we worry about everyone's health. We worry about worrying too much!

Learning that we can pray for freedom from worry and knowing our Higher Power is working in our lives give us hope that we can change.

With our knowledge that God is present always, we can move through troubling experiences, confident that we'll survive—confident, in fact, that we'll grow from the experience.

Asking God what to do in a certain situation always provides us with a response. We feel so much saner when the torment of anxiety isn't shadowing us.

Living in fear of a crisis controls us mentally and emotionally; we get trapped in negativity, perceiving our experiences as threatening even when they aren't. The expectation of a crisis can even trigger one if we're too focused on negative events.

When we begin turning to God to see us through every difficult circumstance, we will discover freedom from fear.

What might happen tomorrow need not concern us today; God will help us when the time has come. What might transpire next year is way down on God's list too. The experiences we need will occur at their own proper time and with God as director.

I will meditate on God being present with me today. I'll have no worries to hinder my joy.

My Higher Power is as close as my willingness to think of the spirit within me. I won't be worried about any experience today if I use my mind to my advantage.

What's to be gained from believing in a Higher Power? Peace of mind comes first. Knowing that we're not alone, that we have a companion to share every burden with, makes any struggle easier to handle.

Nearly every day we ponder what to do about a nagging situation. We review in our minds the "he saids, she saids" until we're worn out, oftentimes still troubled about what to do. And then we remember we have guiding voices all around us. We will listen to our teachers today. No situation has to baffle us.

Surrendering to God,
to the experience, to the moment,
will give me the peace and joy
I long for today.

Today gives me another chance to leave others alone, count my own blessings, and revel in the joy of peacefulness. Peace and sanity are all mine if I want them.

Quieting our minds conserves our energy. In the midst of turmoil, we can get quiet. While trying to make a decision, we can get quiet. When someone is orally attacking us, we can get quiet. When we're close to attacking someone, we can get quiet. When we feel hopeless and unable to go forward, we can get quiet. Peace will come.

Reliving past traumas and projecting future ones tire us almost as much as the actual experiences. We gain nothing from our obsession to dwell on the past and the future. In fact, we lose a lot. We lose the message our Higher Power is trying to give us through the *present* experience when that experience does not capture our full attention.

*I feel calm and guided when
I begin my day in conversation with
God. Remembering that this friend
will never desert me, comforts me.*

Any conflict I get into is because I've forgotten to ask the simple question, "How important is it anyway?" I'll be mindful of this today and stop myself before I get into conflict.

Gratitude releases us from a negative attitude. Deciding to be grateful for our situation, our experiences, our unique perspective, quickly changes our outlook on everything that did happen, on everything that is happening now, and on everyone we meet. Accepting that we are in charge of whatever kind of day we will have forces us to accept responsibility for our joy, which can always be ours, or our unhappiness. And being grateful feels so good.

We need not give up our goals; indeed, we should strive to accomplish them. But when we find doors closing in our faces or get repeated rejections for our efforts, we need to look to our Higher Power for understanding. Perhaps our direction is not consistent with God's will. Surrendering, then, becomes the solution. And the right goal for us will emerge. Getting on track with God will assure us peaceful well-being.

Today I will notice how God has been present in my life. Being quiet will open a channel to that knowledge.

Accepting God's will is all
I need to do today. I won't feel
alone. I will be safe every minute.

Our fears diminish when we know that God is in charge and that our journey is according to Divine design. Our assignment is simply to listen and learn and pass on to others what we've been taught.

My life will be both simple and peaceful today if I let God take charge of others.

If I begin to worry today,
I'll know that I have forgotten
that God is and will always be
my protector. All is well.

My Higher Power has saved me thus far.
I am confident that I will be protected today, too.

Coming to believe that the future as well as the present is in God's hands relieves us of the *need* to worry. However, giving up worry is not easy. It has become second nature to us, yet with dedicated practice we can give it up.

Wringing our hands over another person's behavior never helps the situation. Neither does nagging, at least not for long. Our interference, in even the most subtle ways, won't guarantee the outcome we're certain is best. At times it feels as if we have no recourse. But we always have one: prayer.

Remembering that God's grace has brought us to this point can relieve us of the compulsion to worry about the future.

Today is all there is right now. We are in good hands right now. Tomorrow will take care of itself when it becomes right now.

Deciding that every experience can be interpreted as good is no more difficult than believing the cards are stacked against us. It's a matter of outlook, and no one controls it for us. We are in charge of our outlook. We can seek the humor or the lesson in situations, or we can feel victimized. We can't change the situation, but we can respond to it however we decide.

Quieting our hearts and our minds to receive God's guidance relieves us of pressure we may not have realized was there. We grow used to carrying too many burdens, trying to control too many outcomes. If we choose to be humble—that is, willing to give up our burdens to God—we will be in for difficult yet rewarding times: difficult in that we can no longer be sure events and people will turn out according to our plan; rewarding in that we can look forward to the best outcome for all concerned.

Joy is not exclusively held by a few.

Each of us can find it, feel it,

savor it, maintain it,

and give it away.

I will give my worries to God today. I want my mind free so I can be creative and joyful. I want to laugh and feel grateful.

Hazelden Publishing is a division of the Hazelden Foundation, a not-for-profit organization. Since 1949, Hazelden has been a leader in promoting the dignity and treatment of people afflicted with the disease of chemical dependency.

The mission of the foundation is to improve the quality of life for individuals, families, and communities by providing a national continuum of information, education, and recovery services that are widely accessible; to advance the field through research and training; and to improve our quality and effectiveness through continuous improvement and innovation.

Stemming from that, the mission of this division is to provide quality information and support to people wherever they may be in their personal journey—from education and early intervention, through treatment and recovery, to personal and spiritual growth.

Although our treatment programs do not necessarily use everything Hazelden publishes, our bibliotherapeutic materials support our mission and the Twelve Step philosophy upon which it is based. We encourage your comments and feedback.

The headquarters of the Hazelden Foundation are in Center City, Minnesota. Additional treatment facilities are located in Chicago, Illinois; Newberg, Oregon; New York, New York; Plymouth, Minnesota; and St. Paul, Minnesota. At these sites, we provide a continuum of care for men and women of all ages. Our Plymouth facility is designed specifically for youth and families.

For more information on Hazelden, please call **1-800-257-7800.** Or you may access our World Wide Web site on the Internet at **www.hazelden.org**.